SCAN THIS KEY WITH YOUR MOBILE APP TO UNLOCK THE BOOK

DON'T HAVE THE APP?

Download your app at:

incredebooks.com/disney

ISBN 978-0-9937669-78

Published by Mercury InPress Inc.
53 Auriga Drive, Ottawa, ON, Canada K2E 8C3

For additional information and permissions, please contact Mercury InPress Inc.

www.mercuryinpress.com

PRINTED IN CANADA

TURN TO LAST PAGE FOR INSTRUCTIONS

Mickey and Donald's Rhyme Time

An Interactive Rhyming Story for New Readers

By J.D. Franes

Illustrated by Loter, Inc.

My name is Mickey.
Donald needs my advice.
He's writing a poem
That's just gotta sound nice.

He's trying to write
A poem for Daisy.
But finding words that rhyme
Is driving him crazy.

He spent the whole weekend
Thinking big rhyming thoughts,
But he's still written nothing.
No poems. No plots.

Goofy has a good word.

It rhymes beautifully with dog.

But how sweet is a poem

About a slimy green frog?

Minnie thinks a pretty poem
Would really be better.
Can Donald write about rainbows,
Flowers, or weather?

So Donald needs great words
That make Daisy smile.
But which words are best?
Donald thinks for a while.

Yes, Daisy likes roses.

She loves a nice hat.

He needs rhymes for those words.

Toodles can help him with that.

Oh, Toodles. Oh, Toodles.
I'm certain you've heard,
We need a good hat rhyme.
Can you give us a word?

Rat, gnat, and splat rhymes
Won't make Daisy smile.
We need better words
Full of color and style.

Donald tried really hard
And worked a long time.
But the really sad news is
He claims he can't rhyme.

"You must do this," I said.
"You can't make her wait."
So Donald wrote this poem,
And I think that it's great.

Daisy is my neighbor.
Yes, Daisy's quite a duck.
She's been a friend for many years.
I think that's my good luck.

INSTRUCTIONS

DOWNLOAD

Get your Apple or
Android mobile app from
incredebooks.com/disney

READ

Look for symbols in the
bottom corners of special
book pages.

PLAY

Scan the special page
with your mobile app and
bring it to life in 3D.

Hold your mobile device over
special book pages to activate them.

For more information visit **incredebooks.com**

Incredebooks!™